#

SCHOLARSHIP

SCHOLARSHIP

TWO CONVOCATION ADDRESSES
∽ ON UNIVERSITY LIFE ∾

ABRAHAM KUYPER
TRANSLATED BY HARRY VAN DYKE

Christian's LIBRARY PRESS

GRAND RAPIDS · MICHIGAN

Originally published as *Scolastica, of 't geheim van echte studie.*
© Amsterdam: J. A. Wormser, 1889

Originally published as *Scolastica II. Om het zoeken of om het vinden?
Of het doel van echte studie.*
© Amsterdam / Pretoria: Boekhandel voorheen
[formerly] Höveker & Wormser, 1900

ISBN: 978-1-938948-85-5

Christian's Library Press
An imprint of the Acton Institute for the Study of Religion & Liberty
98 E. Fulton Street
Grand Rapids, Michigan 49503
www.clpress.com

Cover design by Sharon VanLoozenoord
Interior design by Sharon VanLoozenoord
Additional editing by Stephen J. Grabill, Mel Flikkema,
Timothy J. Beals, and Paul J. Brinkerhoff

23 22 21 20 19 18 17 16 15 14   1 2 3 4 5 6 7 8 9 10

Printed in the United States of America

CONTENTS

1
SCOLASTICA I
The Secret of Genuine Study

2
SCOLASTICA II
The Goal of Genuine Study: To Seek or To Find?

FOREWORD

Religious liberty has long been considered one of the hallmarks of modern constitutional democracies. In order to promote and preserve this, many nations intentionally seek to foster religious tolerance among their youth via publicly funded education. Hence, in the United States most public schools intentionally ignore all religious perspectives about the topic of instruction, and thus model for young people how to set aside particular beliefs when participating in public conversation. This method promotes religious tolerance by privatizing religion. Still other schools seek to promote religious tolerance within the overarching narrative that all religions are valid and true. This second method promotes religious tolerance by denying any significant conflict between religions.

For more than one hundred years now, the Netherlands school system has actively fostered religious tolerance in a very different manner. Instead of privatizing religion, the Dutch have recognized that knowledge (curriculum) and behavior (pedagogy) is embedded in core beliefs about the nature of God, humanity, and the world. Hence, Abraham Kuyper and his followers began a decades-long struggle for the establishment and the government financing of confessional schools on the primary and secondary levels. The passage of legislation in 1889 provided partial financial support for confessional schools. Later, the De Visser Act of 1920 provided equal treatment and funding for all schools and created the situation in which each confessional community could establish its own school system. All schools were granted equal access to public funds.

The translation of Abraham Kuyper's *Scolastica I* and *II* anticipates the publication of a larger collection of Kuyper's writings on education under the imprint of Christian's Library Press and by the generous support of Rimmer DeVries and the Acton Institute. The complete volume will include Kuyper's important essay entitled "Bound to the Word," which discusses the topic of what being bound to the Word of God means within the entire world of human thought. The complete volume will also include extracts from important parliamentary speeches by Kuyper on the subject of education, plus a translation of Kuyper's fifteen articles that appeared in his daily newspaper in 1880 under the title "Antirevolutionary Also in Your Household." Appended to this series was a sixteenth article entitled "De School" in which Kuyper discussed the significance of the life of the primary school for the state. Additional essays and speeches in this anthology include parts of Kuyper's 1875 "De schoolkwestie," parts of the 1885 "Ijzer en leem," Kuyper's speech in 1903 to the Christian Teacher's Association, and additional material on Kuyper's views on vouchers.

The above is only a partial listing of the components of this groundbreaking anthology. This forthcoming, larger collection by no means exhausts Kuyper's educational reflections. It will, however, make available in English a substantial amount of the thought on education by one of the most dynamic figures of the late nineteenth and early twentieth centuries.

MEL FLIKKEMA

A NOTE BY THE TRANSLATOR

This small volume contains the texts of two convocation addresses that Abraham Kuyper gave in his function as rector of the *Vrije Universiteit* (Free University) in Amsterdam.

In 1889, and again in 1900, it was Professor Kuyper's turn to act as rector for that year (the office rotated among members of the faculty). At the start of the academic year he used the occasion each time to give fatherly advice to the students on how to study effectively and how to lead the life of a student in a wholesome way. At the same time he sought to inspire them by expounding on the guiding principles of the university they had chosen to attend.

In an engaging way Kuyper shares his view of the divine purpose of scholarship for human culture, and his conviction of the task of the *Vrije Universiteit* to be what he calls an "Opposition School." At its start in 1880, the university had been, in the words of Kuyper himself, "embarrassingly small to the point of blushing"; and twenty years later it was still an embarrassment in terms of size: a small student body, taught by half a dozen professors. Nevertheless, the rector believed their university had every right to exist. After all, it based itself on a centuries-old worldview and stood for a viable alternative to the reigning paradigms of the day.

These talks show Kuyper in two very special roles. He is the patient mentor who seeks to mobilize the younger generation of his constituency for the culture war of his time. And he is the devoted professor who identifies with his students and wants them to succeed. Acting in these roles, he treats weighty topics with a light touch and presents his sometimes surprising insights with incisive analysis sprinkled with humor and common sense. The two addresses can still inspire us today even as they must have inspired his audience over a century ago.

Brief editorial notes have been added throughout in order to identify persons, schools of thought, or events mentioned in the original that might be unfamiliar to contemporary readers. The original text included only two footnotes (both in *Scolastica II*). One of these, a quotation by G. E. Lessing, has been integrated into the text proper, and the source citations have been brought up to contemporary bibliographic standards.

I want to thank Al Wolters and Johan Zwaan for their help with the Greek and Latin.

HARRY VAN DYKE
Winter 2014

ACKNOWLEDGMENTS

The Abraham Kuyper Translation Society, along with Acton Institute and Kuyper College, gratefully acknowledges the financial support and leadership received from Calvin College, Fuller Theological Seminary, Mid-America Reformed Seminary, and the Andreas Center for Reformed Scholarship and Service at Dordt College in the translation of Abraham Kuyper's seminal three-volume work on common grace (*De gemeene gratie*).

SCOLASTICA I

THE SECRET
OF GENUINE STUDY

Esteemed Students,

On behalf of the senate of this University, welcome to our academic auditorium, whether you are a returning student or a new recruit. The oppressive summer heat at times made the atmosphere too sultry to demand much exertion from your brains, but now that the air is becoming cooler your head too is gradually clearing up and the joy of study excites you with renewed urgency. Our friend Bruin the bear busies himself in the summer and goes to sleep when winter approaches, but your lifestyle is exactly the opposite. You take it easy in the summer, but when the sky rises and the thermometer sinks you enter your true element.

I still recall from my own student days how the start of a new academic year beckoned us. In June we yearned to get away. Our head was tired, the courses finished, our wallet usually empty. This couldn't go on. The arrival of a long summer vacation was an exhilarating prospect. To quit the stuffy city and enter the country, to leave the solitary room and travel home, no more lectures, no more exams, master of our own time! How we would enjoy "home sweet home" and drink of the pleasures of life.

In June, yes, those summer holidays opened up visions of true bliss. But then, when June was behind us and July had passed and August had gone by, the best days were over and memories of the good, happy days in the academy rekindled in our imagination. The holidays seemed empty and without purpose. No, this could not go on either. At last we longed for the end of summer and the start of a new school year.

And when the day finally arrived that we returned to our alma mater and the lecture halls and got reacquainted with our fellow students, then we looked with affection even upon our professors behind the lecterns and were happy to see them back, the men who had made us slave away at their courses and who during oral exams had looked like veritable inquisitors. We realized keenly that the university was our real life and that the academy was our real element. Enthusiastically, as though from now on it would be clear sailing and we would hit the books like never before, we embarked on the new semester without a care in the world and hungry for more knowledge.

I hope that all you returning students have come back with similar feelings. At the end of the holidays a student is like a fish on dry land, and to greet the academy again is for him to meet the flood tide that surrounds him, lifts him up, and bathes him in fresh waters. As for you first-year students, you may not be familiar with such delights, but you will experience even greater riches. To become a university student for the first time is for you to enter into a new, mysterious world, a world that fascinates you precisely because it is so mysterious.

So greetings and welcome to you all, whether you are already acquainted with these riches or will experience them for the first time.[1] Let there be a tremor of noble intentions in your hearts! Open your eyes wide and muster all your strength to really study hard this time. We your professors, we too have our hearts beat-

---

1   The Free University (*Vrije Universiteit*) at this time (1889) had 80 students and 5 professors. The University had first opened its doors in Amsterdam in 1880.

ing more rapidly now that we see you back. A lot is expected again of you and of us. Much will be demanded again from all of us this year. Very well, let us resume our task with manly courage and Christian sense. And in case difficulties await us, let us begin not with presumption but in humility. For our help is in the name of the Lord who made the heavens and the earth and therefore also made the world of thought and for that thought the world of study.

———— ⚬✸⚬ ————

If by way of introduction to that study I now offer you some words about the nature of study, please give me your still undivided attention for what I am going to say about the *disciplina scolastica*. If you were not students I would add: don't let the sound of the word *scolastica* frighten you just because it reminds you of nothing so much as arid concepts and overly subtle distinctions. But a university student does not go by the sound of a word and old specters do not frighten him. In the word *scolastica* you detected the root *scola* and so you understood immediately that the *vita scolastica* is the life of the school and has nothing to do with the disputations of the old scholastics. Yet even then you do not reach deep enough for its meaning. *Scola* is not a school of *learning*. *Scola* is the *res publica litterarum*, the entire republic of letters, that distinctive sphere in society which indeed centers on the university yet pervades the country with young men who thirst after knowledge and with men of learning who illumine our towns and villages like bright stars.[2]

2　The first Dutch woman to earn a university degree was Aletta Jacobs in 1878, at the City University of Amsterdam. The Free University of Amsterdam opened its doors to a female student in 1905; however, she did not graduate, and not till 1918 did a number of young women again enroll. See Arie Theodorus van Deursen, *The Distinctive Character of the Free University in Amsterdam, 1880–2005: A Commemorative History*, trans. Herbert Donald Morton (Grand Rapids: Eerdmans, 2008), 83.

In 1619, our Reformed polyhistor Alstedt[3] dedicated a marvelous book to the States General.[4] It was a book of more than four thousand columns that saved a poor student the cost of acquiring a library since this single quarto served as a handbook for *all* the subjects. It was a library in itself. It even contained a Hebrew, Greek, and Latin lexicon, nor did it omit a manual for music. But, what I wanted to get to, in this quarto Alstedt also dealt with *Ethica*, and after completing it he says that he will now move on to *Symbiotica*, that is, to the science of symbiosis or living together, of which there are, he says, three in number. There are three spheres in life each drawn with their own compass: *Economica*, *Politica* and *Scolastica*. *Economica*, that is the science of domestic life; *Politica*, that is the science of the life of the state; and then follows *Scolastica*, that is the science of the republic of letters, or if you will, of the circle of scholars.

In those good old days, all those who devoted themselves to scholarship or completed a classical education were regarded as constituting a separate life-sphere, a distinct order in society.

People were still aware that men of science[5] lived by a distinctive principle, moved in a separate world, and were called by God to fulfill a special task in the whole of human society.

A professor would therefore address his students as *ornatissimi commilitones*: distinguished comrades, fellow conscripts in the army corps to which he himself belonged, companions in the war against the same enemy, in the service of the same country.

---

3 Johann Heinrich Alstedt (1588–1638), professor of philosophy and theology at Herborn in the duchy of Nassau, Germany, and later in Transylvania, which at the time was an independent principality with a strong presence of Calvinists.

4 Governing body of delegates representing the United Provinces of the Netherlands (Dutch Republic; 1579–1795), called the parliament, consisting of a First (upper) and a Second (lower) Chamber, but not to be confused with the present Netherlands parliament of the same name.

5 Throughout, Kuyper writes "wetenschap," which is a very inclusive term in Dutch comprehending the arts and humanities as well as the natural and social sciences. Depending on the context, this translation renders the term by turns as "science," "scholarship," "knowledge," "learning," or "erudition."

This was already understood in ancient Israel. Men of learning were regarded as a separate family, where every teacher was called "father" and his pupils were greeted as spiritual "sons." You know those names "father" and "sons" from the wisdom of the writer of Proverbs. That awareness of having a distinctive calling in life and a special God-given task—how gloriously it speaks to you when you read there: "My son, if you receive my words and treasure up my commandments with you, making your ear attentive to *wisdom* and inclining your heart to *understanding;* yes, if you call out for *insight* and raise your voice for *understanding,* if you seek it like *silver* and search for it as for hidden *treasures,* then you will understand the fear of the LORD and find the *knowledge of God.* For the LORD gives wisdom; from his mouth come knowledge and understanding; he stores up sound wisdom for the upright; he is a shield to those who walk in integrity."[6]

This was originally the basis on which rested the whole concept of a university, for it did not denote then what was made of it later, a *universitas scientiarum,* a community of the sciences. Rather, it had an altogether different meaning: a university was a *universitas docentium et discentium,* a community of teachers and learners united in a single corporate body. That is why men spoke of a "republic of letters" as a commonwealth that transcended all states and empires and formed its own sphere throughout the world. That was also the particular reason why this republic had its own language: not the Latin of Cicero but a Latin which it had itself forged out of the old Roman tongue.

True, this high and holy conception of a university was soon falsified. Young men whose object was not the study itself nevertheless coveted the privileges attached to the order of the learned and began to penetrate our sacred garden like veritable parasites. And then the sense of constituting a separate order bred stupid and foolish self-exaltation that stamped everyone whose name

---

6   Prov. 2:1–7.

but appeared on the registrar's rolls as a *scholar*, while everyone who did not belong to the elect, to the "men of the gown," was booed and reviled as a *philistine* or a "man of the town." Especially when the order of scholars still had external privileges and could with impunity defy the "constables" during nightly raids on shop signs and doorbells, and when a student paid no import duty on his wine, then privilege, as everywhere else so here, worked its evil effect. Not studying but creating a nuisance in public and carousing and drinking their buddies under the table became the base occupation in which students sought their honor. And of course, from their student days this false pride accompanied them into life. Because they had once attended university they thought they could forever look down with contempt on all those who had never gone to university. The holy laurels of learning fell into the mire, and the renegades' mugs were wreathed in the vines of wild creepers.

This behavior came home to roost, and the outcome was that the sphere of scholarship lost its native impulse, tore up its charter, and put itself in the service of the State, so that *Scolastica* dissolved into *Politica*. Worse, a desire to break down the faith instead of shoring it up became for many the principal motive for doing scholarship. At last the evil, narrow-minded selfishness arrived that sees no higher purpose in the academy than to assist its visitors as quickly as possible in preparing them for what is called a "position." The first stage caused the academy to forfeit its freedom, the second set it in opposition to God, and the third lowered it to the level of "studying to pass the exams." And who knows, maybe they have also sneaked into our own university already—those young men who supposedly are devoting themselves to academic studies but who have only one goal in mind: once and for all, and as quickly and cheaply as possible, to be done with bookish learning. They are parasites who come in order to pursue "success" but whose parched lips have never tasted one draught from the holy grail of scholarship. They are not looking for silver and do not search for hidden gold in the mine of scholarship: their only goal is to acquire a steady position and a guaranteed salary.

Do you see now why I wanted to talk about *Scolastica*? At the start of the new year I wanted to put this question to you before the face of God: What should be the goal of university study and the goal of living and working in the sacred domain of scholarship? I wanted to see whether I might perhaps rouse in some of you a more sanctified passion.

To have the opportunity of studying is such an inestimable privilege, and to be allowed to leave the drudgery of society to enter the world of scholarship is such a gracious decree of our God. Nature out there (God's Word says: as a punishment for sin) is hard for 99 percent of the human race. Of the 1,400 million people who live on this earth there are at least 1,300 million who literally have to eat their bread "by the sweat of their brow"—on farm or factory, at lathe or anvil, in shop or office, forever occupied in wresting food, clothing, and shelter from nature by processing, shaping, shipping, or selling it. And the real man of science does not look upon this with contempt. On the contrary, he senses that to live such a life should really have been his lot too, and that he, bowing under God's ordinances if that were his occupation, would have found happiness and honor in it. But God created, in addition to the world of nature with all its elements and forces and materials, a *world of thoughts*; for all of creation contains Λόγος [Logos]. You are familiar with what the apostle John testifies in the opening of his gospel: "ἐν ἀρχῇ ἦν ὁ Λόγος . . . και δι᾽ αὐτοῦ τὰ πάντα ἐγένετο καὶ χωρὶς αὐτοῦ ἐγένετο οὐδὲ ἕν ὃ γέγογεν."[7]

Now the deeper meaning of this Λόγος is only disclosed to us through the revelation of God's mystery. He who does not worship God as the Triune One does not understand this mystery. But even if for now we do not try to remove the curtain from this holy place

---

7   "In the beginning was the Word . . . and through him all things were made and without him nothing was made that has been made." Cf. John 1:1, 3. Kuyper appears to be quoting from memory.

of worship, this at least is clear: there is not only a creation but also a Λόγος in the creation, and man, created in the image of God and therefore a logical creature, has the capacity and the calling to use his logical thought to reflect upon this Λόγος which shines in all creation. And this, students, is the beautiful, exalted, sacred task of science.

Now if nature were not so hard and life not so cruel, many more people could have the enjoyment of that sacred calling. But things being what they are, only a few are granted that honor and by far most people are deprived of that privilege.

But you and I have received this great favor from our God. We belong to that specially privileged group. Thus, woe to you and shame on you if you do not hear God's holy call in the field of scholarship and do not exult with gratitude and never-ending praise that it pleased God out of free grace to choose you as his instrument for this noble, uplifting, inspiring calling.

It is for God's honor that there should be scholarship in the land. His thought, his Λόγος in the κόσμος [kosmos], must not remain unknown and unexamined. He created us as logical beings in order that we should trace his Λόγος, investigate it, publish it, personally wonder at it, and fill others with wonder. This too proclaims the glory of his name. Without scientific research that treasure remains hidden in the world and does not rise to the surface. As the Zulu for centuries walked over the goldfields without suspecting what treasures the miners of Transvaal would one day dig up, so too the nonscientific person treads upon the soil of God's creation until the man of science discovers the mine of knowledge, opens it up, descends into it, and searches there for silver, to bring out the gold of God's thoughts.

Of course man can live *without* science and scholarship, witness the native peoples of Botswana, Mongolia, and North America. But not until a higher form of consciousness awakens in people does human life receive its nobility from the thoughts of God. Then man increases his power over nature and moves from the dark cellar to the bright upper room flooded in light.

Thus there are three wonderful things about science: it brings to light the hidden glory of God; it gives you joy in the act of digging up the gold that lies hidden in creation; and it grants you the honor of raising the level and well-being of human life. So whatever made you think that you can become a scholar merely by studying and cramming for exams? No, I tell you, even if you had stuffed your brain full of facts and theories and had passed every examination *summa cum laude,* you would still be no more than a hewer of wood and a drawer of water in this elite corps of scholars if you had not entered that world of God's thoughts with all your heart and all your mind and if in that world of God's glorious thoughts you had not heard the voice of him who had ordained you a priest of learning and anointed you with consecrated oil for that holy priesthood.

Every man of learning should be fired with a zeal to battle *against* the darkness and *for* the light. The glow of gas lay hidden for centuries in the dark coal mine, but not until that coal was dug from the mine and processed by human art did it reveal its luster. Similarly, it is your high calling to wrest the light of God's splendor from the hidden recesses of creation, not in order to seek honor for yourself but honor for your God.

To be sure, God has caused light to rise in our darkness also along avenues other than science. His is not the cruelty of our age that allowed generation after generation to wander in darkness until at last in this nineteenth century the lights could go on—and then only for the aristocracy of the intellect. God is gracious and compassionate, and by means of his revelation and the founding of his church he had from the beginning ignited a glow that faith imbibed and that enriched an Abraham and a Moses far beyond what any nineteenth-century learning is capable of—rich in their heart, rich in their soul, rich in those more tender sensations that bear the mark of the eternal. And scholars, far from being able to do without that faith, must begin by being rich in that faith if they are ever to feel their heart stir with the holy impulse that drives them to engage in true scholarship.

Still, scholarship is something all its own—not something higher, but a work of our minds whereby the minds travel along other paths. Even if there were no salvation for sinners and if God's wrath plunged us all into eternal perdition, even then our race would not be absolved from the obligation to investigate the Logos that God has hidden in his creation and to bring it to light. God must not be robbed of this honor. Science is bound to religious belief only to the extent that an unbelieving man of science causes science's beehive, as much as depends on him, to degenerate into a wasps' nest. He does this unintentionally, simply because he cannot act otherwise, in order to rob God of that Logos and pass it for a product of his own thoughts. That defines the school of science in this century, which wants to be something outside of God, apart from God, in opposition to God, and to seek its glory in ridiculing the Christian faith. But even this derailed science brings gain, for what it correctly observes *is observed* and what it properly investigates *is investigated*. Nevertheless it contains a dangerous element by wandering off into materialistic science or else by setting its hypotheses in opposition to the θέσις [*thesis*] of God's revelation. Either way, it deviates from its sacred calling to be God's minister, God's priest in his holy temple.

The suggestion that men of faith for this reason would have to flee from the world of science can only be maintained by the unscientific person. For that would amount to forsaking one's duty, abandoning science to unholy secularization, and personally forfeiting the influence that men of faith must exercise on the thinking of our generation. Instead, given this state of affairs, it is imperative—and this will give you a clue as to why the Free University was founded—that a warmer, bolder interest in science and learning should awaken among God's people, in order to get derailed science back on its God-given track and to refute the lie that faith hates science. At the same time we need to be encouraged not to disdain the scholarship of others but together with others to contribute to mankind's great scholarly task, provided only that it can do so in its own institution.

———∞§∞———

But I hear you! I understand your barely concealed laughter asking me whether students are already PhDs and whether I would want to see you parading on Amsterdam's streets, thrusting out your chest and proudly proclaiming, "Here goes a man of science." No, I do not. I would rather that you keep alive the old tradition of dusting off every conceited young man who may have stolen into your ranks. Whoever cures a fellow student of this academic leprosy deserves well of his country. Genius of genuine gold, as Fichte put it so beautifully, does not know its own beauty.[8] Real talent has the fragrance of a flower without being aware of it. The true scientific spirit possesses its ornament with blushing naïveté. Academia nurses little hope for young men who notice too early that they are smart and who leave their village and sail into the university town as prodigies. Indeed, I go further and tell you that a youth who sits in his room calculating whether he might not be made of the stuff that professors are made of should never even have enrolled and should be struck from the registrars' rolls for covert misconduct. I also know very well that no one person can learn all knowledge and that one can sooner empty the North Sea with an oyster shell than that a student with the shell of his brain could drink up the ocean of science. For a single discipline alone, the studies are so voluminous that the successful defense of a dissertation, even if passed *cum laude*, means little more than the declaration that the newly minted *doctor* can now at least begin to realize that he still knows or understands almost nothing. Europe has only one Mont Blanc, and the intellectual world too has ever so many stretches of plains, then broad mountain ranges, and only here and there a lonely Alpine peak. So if the *scola* does not want to decimate itself, it must not use a few men of genius as its standard. That would end in a deluge

---

8 Kuyper refers here to the German philosopher Johann Gottlieb Fichte
(1762–1814).

with barely eight souls in the ark, and also much cattle. No, its rule must embrace the entire body of scholars and so must also be geared to the emergency personnel in the field hospitals. But to study any discipline at all takes such a huge effort that even if you make no higher demand than to be a half-decent participant, there is just no time left to feed the tiniest microbe of self-conceit. Solid study is the natural antidote for those critters, and the remedy never fails.

But if a recruit—say, a child of the regiment—has just joined the colors, that does not yet give him access to the council of war—unless it be to hand a book or a map to the commander. Yet for all that, he is a member of the regiment! And if the next day the entire army is routed and this recruit is the only one left, then the recruit, if he is a man, will pick up the colors and wave it till his last breath; it will not drop from his failing hands until it is captured by the foe.

This is the holy awareness that I wanted to kindle in you students as you enter the fortress of science. For whatever modest place you take up at the back of our corps, you are nevertheless *inside* the boundary that separates the domain of science from what lies outside it. You are recruits, not yet with the marshal's baton in hand, yet fully inducted into the corps. Your aspirations and intentions should merge with the aspirations and intentions of that corps. You are wearing its uniform and therefore the spirit that inspires the corps to victory must not be foreign to your spirit. Just as a commander sins if he risks the battle without lifting up his divine vocation before the face of God, so the conscript is wanting in godliness if he takes up his guard duties without being conscious of the divine nature of his vocation and without praying to God for his blessing. Do I mean that you should pray before opening the pages of Lysias[9] or memorizing the Hebrew alphabet? Most certainly you should do that too, but what I mean

---

9 Lysias (ca. 445–ca. 380 BC) was an Athenian logographer (speech writer) and orator in classical Greece.

reaches deeper. I mean that you place yourself with all your academic hopes and dreams before the face of God in such a way that praying for your studies flows naturally from it and is not attached to it as an afterthought. What I ask of you is that you realize something of the reason why God for the sake of his work wants there to be scientific learning among men; that you begin to see how on account of sin *only a few* are elected to be engaged in scholarship at various levels as a calling from God; that you will be jubilant with praise and thanksgiving for being privileged to take your place among the ranks of the elect; and that you will be impressed from the outset with the fearful thought that every person who has received this as his calling can only say that his study is wasted and his life lost if he dies without *having contributed his share to the honor of God*. Or, to say it with an allusion to a word of our Lord: I want you students to realize that the man with the spade and the man of the leather apron, if they have thought about their vocation, will enter the kingdom of God before you.

This is not to suggest that someday you should all write fat tomes or advance the frontiers of science. Only the peaks above the snow line form lasting glaciers; what lies at lower levels melts anyway. Yet each of you has the calling to *live life* as a scholar and to gather honey for the great beehive of life in the interest of the surroundings in which you will eventually be placed. A single educated man in a humble village is for that village the hub of a higher life. A scholar's mission in life should be to serve and not to be served. Our maxim will always be: "Freely ye have received, freely give."[10] Indeed, the point is that you are open to *receive*, that you are receptive. Not necessarily so that you may receive *much*. The rock shelf where the waterfall clatters down *receives* less than the loose, sandy soil that is normally watered from the clouds by droplets only.

---

10 Matt. 10:8 KJV.

The "receiving" that leads to *knowing* is expressed etymo-
logically in almost all languages with a metaphor derived from
procreation. The unchaste woman becomes a mother only by ac-
cident; the whore as a rule dies childless; only the chaste, re-
spectable woman conceives and so *receives*. But that is exactly
why you are required to embrace science in love, why your blood
should stir passionately for science, and why you should be rav-
ished by her beauty not in the marketplace but in discrete pri-
vacy. In your mind lies your glory as scholars. That is your field of
labor. Not merely to live, but to know *that* you live and *how* you
live, and how things around you live, and how all that hangs together and lives out of the one efficient cause that proceeds from
God's power and wisdom. Other people, when evening falls, have
to have sown and plowed, counted and calculated; but you have
to have *thought, reflected, analyzed,* until at last a harvest of
your own thoughts may germinate and ripen on the field of your
consciousness.

You too for your part must feel called to be a nurseryman
in this consecrated garden. And if others plant a cedar or a vine
while you perhaps make only cuttings of lilac or hyssop, that
does not matter. Even mint, dill, and cumin belong to the plant
world. Just as long as *something* is growing, and as long as that
something is not a *weed*.

And how does this sense of calling become evident? To begin with, if study is your delight or if it is your burden. Time for
relaxation may intervene—I would say, *must* intervene. But the
kind of relaxation that you look for marks you. If you are one of
those who, when the books can be pushed aside for a while, seek
recreation by descending hastily to what is base and making up
for lost time by indulging in coarse entertainment or debauchery
and drunken revelry, no, then you are not a man of the colors on
this sacred battlefield but a wretched marauder, and only when
it becomes evident that you seek your relaxation in things noble,
honest, pure, and lovely will you be given your commission for
this holy war.

Your sense of calling also becomes evident when you take up your studies again. For *how* you study is crucial. Is it: first finish the general program to get to your major, then go fishing for the questions usually asked on the oral finals, and then with the diploma in your pocket heave a sigh of relief: "Thank God, I'm done with books for the rest of my life!"—in that case what have you, trained racehorse, divined of God in the study of languages, in mathematics, in the beauties of classical studies, in the finer details of your chosen discipline? Eyes open, you saw nothing; ears open, you heard nothing. You took in ballast, sailed with ballast, and now you throw the ballast overboard. You toured the country in a hooded carriage, took lodging at nightfall in village after village, but now that you have reached your destination you know nothing about the countryside because you saw nothing and observed nothing.

A farmer who has *studied* his draft horse and knows how to handle it is more scientific than a "learned" graduate whose whole academic achievement consists in a scrap of paper that was handed to him upon graduation, a certificate that will accuse his conscience for the rest of his life.

Real study takes time. Not a year, or a year and a half, of frittering away the days, and then like a fireman working up a sweat at the pump. He who has a love of scholarship is like the worker bee that leaves the hive early in the morning, forages for flowers, and comes back in time with honey as its prize. Such a student studies more than what has been assigned for the exam; he loves to crack open a book, wants to get a general education, and picks up, say, the *Iliad* in the original, not in order that he might give a half-baked translation of it if it were ever asked, but to enjoy it for himself because it is beautiful and to get a sense of what it is that makes it so beautiful.

The pseudostudent builds a house of blocks, like a child, and when he has finished it he puts the blocks back in the box. The true student builds a proper house and takes care that his studies are done properly: the beams have to be real beams, the iron bolts of real iron and not of tin, and the cornerstone a real stone that can bear the necessary weight. This causes him to develop a sense of what is truth. Not guessing at it, and by chance coming up with a tolerable answer. Not bragging and showing off with what is not asked and what is not relevant. But really *knowing* what you know. Every argument a genuine argument. Every opinion an opinion that has merit. Checking every link in a chain of ideas to see whether the argument is watertight. After all, the man of science does not play fast and loose with the facts, but it is granted him to track down the gold of God's thoughts, the gems of divine wisdom, a labor that requires real discernment. Then you may at times know much less than the braggart and look shabby next to the dandy; but is the woman who can adorn her throat with one real diamond not richer than the trollop from the music hall who has bedecked her bosom with the glitter of costume jewelry?

―――――― ⸙ ――――――

I pray that this quiet conviction of having a sacred calling may more and more govern your whole academic life! I hope it will govern your relationship *with your professors.* It is the sneak who bows and scrapes before them to avoid difficulties at exam time, and he it is who picks on the "bookish" student as his favorite target for the arrows of his ridicule. The serious student, by contrast, sees in his professors what the soldier values—not in the barracks but on the battlefield—about his officers: men who know a little more than he and can lead him to where he otherwise would never arrive. Professors are not your commanders but your fellow soldiers—the concept *fellow soldiers,* after all, is necessarily reciprocal. They are men whom you don't avoid but seek out. You are not blind to their faults and failings, and you gently poke fun at them in order to improve them; but in the end you know that they share one holy calling with you.

That sense of calling should be no less evident *in student life.* Because we form a *scola* together, a distinctive sphere, a distinctive class in society, the motive for which God called that sphere into being should also govern your social intercourse. A hunter loves to talk about his partridges, his dogs, his adventures at the chase. A mariner will talk about port and starboard, windward and leeward, halyard and bowsprit. A good housewife talks almost too much about her children and her maids. And that is how you will also hear students talk: sometimes about a pretty girl they spotted, yes, or a perfect carambole in billiards; but in general their talk will be a discussion of an issue *in the world of thought*, a skirmish which at times resembles a real fight. Small-town squabbles and petty jealousies will be cut off by their fresh tone and candor. Students state frankly what they think; they tell each other the plain truth. But talk behind someone's back they leave to the "philistines."

Their sense of calling becomes evident even in the way they handle their *money* and take care of their *body*. I know, money is always a student's "weak point," but it makes such a difference if a student, like a hunter his partridge, carries home in triumph the book he won at an auction thanks to a skillful bid, or that if he spends even his book money on fancy shawls or absurdly priced cigars or rides in a fancy carriage. I am not ridiculing anyone's small means; there are students who crave books and feel nostalgic when they look at their empty shelves. But at least they don't squander their money, and that very nostalgia speaks of their love of study.

When I mentioned *care of the body* I was again serious. The apostle Paul already pointed out how the Greek athletes and wrestlers made certain to strengthen their muscles in preparation for the match;[11] and our gymnasts, cyclists, and rowers model for us how a *sensible treatment of the body* enhances the use of their muscles. Now would a student be responsible before God if he thought about everything except his body and thoughtlessly neglected it? Such unholy spiritualism will not get you very far. If

---

11 Cf. 1 Cor. 9:24–27.

you want to be devoted to "things of the spirit," then make sure you don't begin to look like a spirit. If you are called to reflect on how things are interrelated, can you overlook the relation between yourself and your body? And is it not peculiar about our *scola* and your role in it that *study* stands in contrast to *bodily movement* and that it concentrates all your exertions on that part of the body which you call your brains and which controls more powerfully than any other part the well-being of your entire body and can exhaust it through overexertion? That is why you need to make a study of your body. You have to exercise it, you have to keep it fresh. A *sana mens* dwells only in a *sano corpore*.[12] And whoever thinks that fresh air, vigorous movement, nutritious meals, and regular sleep are of secondary importance for scholarship should read Bilderdijk's *Ziekte der geleerden*[13] and be cured of his presumption and madness by this gigantic beacon at sea.

Your *method* of studying, too, must be inspired and directed by that sense of being enlisted in the world of scholarship. You are to build, and building demands a structured course of action. No futile Sisyphus labor, in which the rock, rolled uphill, forever rolls down again. No pointless task as of the Danaids, filling jars riddled with holes so that the water flows out again as fast as it is collected. Look at lambs skipping in the meadow, how they go about rehearsing in a fashion. If you keep on studying without ever rehearsing and reviewing, in the end you will know nothing. You have to be methodical about your study. Scientific study, if nothing else, must be approached scientifically. Don't just work, but think about *how* you work. Why this and not that? Why this first and that later? Don't just work through the books on your shelf, but proceed as demanded by your ability to absorb, in keeping with the organic interconnectedness of knowledge.

---

12 These Latin phrases are from the original "Orandum est ut sit mens sana in corpore sano," a line found in the Roman poet Juvenal, *Satires* (bk. 10, line 356), translated "A man should pray for a healthy mind in a healthy body."

13 Willem Bilderdijk, *The Disease of Scholars* (Amsterdam en 's Gravenhage: Johannes Allart en gebr. Van Cleef, 1807). This is a didactic poem in six cantos.

Read widely, but remember that mere browsing yields knowledge that evaporates quickly. So, if you manage your time and know how to make the most of your hours and minutes, you will double your work time and have more free time to boot. The watchword of science is *order*. If you study chaotically you will get lost in the chaos. They are mountain climbers, not loafers and drifters, who have taught us, *Qui va piano va sano é qui va sano va lontano*.[14]

Finally I come to *form*. By itself, I agree, form and design belong to the world of art; but the world of science too calls for the beauty of design. Consider the Father of lights! Is his creation ever without design, and do the smallest leaf and the tiniest insect not display the most artful finishing touches? So would it be proper for the scholarly elite to view the requirements of form as falling beneath their dignity and to regard the restrictions of design as undermining their freedom and independence? I realize that sensitivity to design is not given to everyone equally, so I will not insist that every student's digs be tastefully furnished and that the cut of everybody's coat be well tailored. But there is one demand that comes to all students without exception: that you pay attention to outward form. The ancient lesson *Non scolae sed vitae*[15] means that each of you in your own way, as men of learning, will soon have to take up a position in society in order to serve, bless, inspire your fellow man, which you cannot do if you neglect the form. Form and design are the hydraulic drills with which you penetrate the public with what you have to say. Suppose two men appear before the bench, at the lectern, on the pulpit, on a dais, or in a panel, one of whom is less talented yet whose appearance is pleasant, whose thoughts flow clearly, whose style and diction are refined, whose voice is pleasing, whose enunciation is pure, whose manner of speaking is compelling, and whose gestures are

---

14 This Latin phrase means slow and steady wins the race.

15 This Latin phrase is translated, "[We learn] not for the school but for life," an inversion of the original phrase *Non vitae sed scholae discimus*, by which Roman philosopher Seneca (ca. 4 BC–AD 65) meant to reproach armchair philosophers. Lucius Annaeus Seneca, *Epistulae morales ad Lucilium*, Epistula 106.

well timed, then this man of few talents will have far greater influence that the man of ten talents who is carelessly dressed, has a poor style, speaks with an accent, has an awkward posture and waves his arms like a windmill. Outward form is therefore crucial. You cannot dispense with it; your success, your future, your influence depend on it. Proper form will determine whether you will waste your time and energy in the world of science or make a lasting contribution to it; that is, whether you will answer to your God-given calling or forsake that calling. Of course I know that form can be hollow, artificial, false. God preserve you from it. But may God also preserve you from that levity that thinks: "The form will take care of itself." That may be true for men of genius, but to those of you who are modest enough not to fancy yourself a genius I say: devote some time to studying these things, in the knowledge that it is no less true of form and design that *pour savoir quelque chose, il faut l'avoir appris.*[16]

———— ⚬❀⚬ ————

I have come to the end of my address and go back to where I began. The *scola*—or, if you prefer, the circle of people with an academic education—is a God-ordained order in society by virtue of a divine calling. If you keep that in mind you know that it implies pure living and sincere piety. Scholarship is not abstract learning separate from life. The saying that "great men have great faults" only reminds us, also in academia, that great powers of genius and talent have been lost for service in the temple of science through pride and dissoluteness. Brilliant minds and sharp intellects may impress you, but if moral truth is absent so also will be the unction of priestly love and dedication. Τὸ ἀληθές [*To alēthes*] and τὸ ἀγαθόν [*to agathon*] cannot be separated.[17] Whoever fails to honor God's laws in the temple of science only raises clouds

---

16 This French phrase means to know something, you have to have studied it.

17 I.e., the true and the good are inseparable.

of dust that darken his view of truth. So live clean lives and hate what is base and immoral. Light does not illumine the field of science except for the righteous—provided, and I would emphasize this, provided it is not the righteousness of the Stoic but the tender purity of the child of God. Only from faith does the spark fly upward that lights the passion for science in your breast—the faith which feeds on God's revelation and submits to it, and which personally gives you the blissful knowledge that you are a child of God; but as applied to the *scola*, also a faith that makes you serve the Lord of glory in your studies and gives you the unshakable conviction that God *elected* you for these studies. To have the *cor ecclesiae*, the doctrine of election, applied to your studies is the goal of every Reformed university. Not even the least among the brothers may say, "I am a reject," and even if you did not choose this life yourself but had it chosen for you by your parents, still you will hold fast to the calling of your God despite this *mediated* decision. It is he who has ordained your life for this order, this sphere, this academic world, and woe betide you if you stop your ears to this call or resist it. He called you by name, and you have only to answer: "Lo, here I am" and to be faithful in this service of your God till your last breath.

Students, let this faith set the tone as we embark on a new year. No doubt disappointment awaits us also this time, but the blood of the Mediator has atoned for sin also in the world of science and scholarship. Only take care never to do one thing: to give up on your ideal. In your studies, always leave your calling the way God has ordained it and do not spoil it in accordance with your own limited ideas.

I thank you.

SCOLASTICA II

THE GOAL OF GENUINE STUDY: TO SEEK OR TO FIND?

Aestumattissimi, Ornatissimi Commilitones,

Latin may be dying out but allow me to address you according to academic tradition as *Distinguished Students, Esteemed Comrades-in-arms,* and to bid you once more, on behalf of the senate, a warm welcome in the army camp of our studies. Welcome first of all to you upperclassmen as you rejoin the colors for a new campaign, but just as warm a welcome to you first-year students, fresh recruits from the gymnasia, presenting yourselves for the first time under the university banner. "Going home" at the end of the academic year may elicit rich sensations of relaxation, especially if you've earned your leave after passing your courses. Nevertheless, come autumn, a longing for our academic army tent rekindles your fighting spirit. And that our novices yearned to join our ranks is all the more understandable at a university where no dread of malicious initiation rites comes to deflate high expectations and where proper modesty ensures a safe-conduct against any molestation at the periphery.

Thus the start of a new school year always makes for a positive mood in our circles. Also among us, your professors. We have dedicated our lives to the struggle for a sacred principle. It is our passion to hunt down the lie in the world of academic scholarship and to dislodge error from its hiding place. After a period of rest, the parole to press onward burns on our lips. It is like a brook that swells and wants to flood the fields. And what scene can be more desirable, what sight more striking, than to see you all lined up again in front of us, eager to listen to our words if well-founded.

Students, we are supposed to form you; but you in turn form us. As the child makes a woman into a mother, so the student makes the professor. Time and again your curiosity elicits from us what might otherwise never have passed our lips, and for all our delight in inspiring you, you also inspire us. As well, our hearts are still somewhat heavy when we contemplate our small numbers, and although the sexagenarians among us are not yet ready to retire, still we feel we need assistance, soon replacement.[1] Without new recruits an elite corps dies out. And where else but from your midst are they to come who will before long take our place? That is why you are *spes nostra*—our hope. Today you are our listeners, tomorrow the mouthpieces of our word, and someday—this is our quiet prayer—more than just our epigones.[2]

Spes nostra, but no less *spes patriae*, the hope of our country. For the spirit of our forefathers that has taken hold of us continues to meet with hostile resistance among the leading circles of our nation. And although our faithful God still spared a remnant, that remnant cannot strive for victory, can barely hold its own, and will be defenseless if it does not acquire, *also outside the church*, heroic men who can bear arms in every domain: the one the sling and the bow, the other the sword and the lance. Our Christian folk are crying out for such men; they hope to see such men come forth from among you in ever larger numbers. And if our people

---

1 The Free University at this time (1900) had 6 professors, 126 students, and 3 departments (theology, law, and letters).

2 I.e., more than just our followers or imitators.

give generously to our school and have given our Free University the love of their hearts, then it is because they expect us to teach you the indispensable skills, and for the brightest among you the fundamentals of military science, for waging our sacred struggle.

All the more do we trust that this high-minded expectation will not be disappointed because your passing up other universities and choosing to come here in itself already betrays your willingness to make a considerable sacrifice for your principle. Our young institution lacks so much of what is offered in abundance at other schools. Our departments are few, our faculty is pitifully small, we are without academic institutes worthy of the name, and the degrees we confer still lack any *effectus civilis*.[3] To have studied here has never yet been a recommendation for public office; to *dare* to have studied here still bears a mark of obloquy. But that is precisely why your coming here is a *moral* act that compares so favorably with other people's love of ease and abject betrayal of principle. It is the *moral* character of your choice that automatically creates a bond of spiritual kinship between you and your professors and gives real meaning to the title *comrades in arms*. And so long as the flame of that holy principle continues to burn in our breast, our paucity of numbers cannot discourage us and the heat of day does not daunt us.

Nevertheless, students, studying at an Opposition School need not be made more onerous than necessary. It borders on cruelty to strew your difficult path with stumbling block after stumbling block, and in this opening address I am therefore going to try and remove at least one of those nasty obstacles. Or is it not offensive, and is it not calculated to dampen all your courage, when you put up with sacrifices and then to hear them yell at you from the opposite side: "You won't find scholarship at the Free

---

3 To lack "civil effect" meant that a degree in law or letters earned at the Free University did not qualify its holders to serve in public offices such as notaries, registered attorneys and justices, or to serve as teachers of the classical languages in the public gymnasia. This disadvantage would be removed by the Higher Education Act piloted through parliament by the Kuyper Ministry in 1905.

University anyway, just indoctrination in time-worn proposi-
tions. Filling station is perhaps too banal a name, but your would-
be university will never be more than a drill school, a cramming
school for regurgitating ancestral lore." This evil accusation,
which is even echoed in the major liberal papers, might easily become too much for you first-year students, too much in any case
for you to be able to respond to it with a principled refutation. You
can stop your ears to it, but that is not how you defeat it. That is
why I am going to use this opportunity to put your mind at ease
on this point at least. If I spoke eleven years ago about the *secret* of genuine study, let me on this occasion speak to you about
the *goal* of genuine study, focusing on the all-important question:
What is the point of scientific study? Is it to seek or to find?

--------⚬⚬⚬--------

The difference between seeking and finding as the goal of
scientific study is best illustrated by pointing to analogies taken
from daily life. You have heard of the recreational activity of the
hunt. What is it that drives all those gentlemen who normally
live a life of ease (a few not even all that steady on their feet ow-
ing to rheumatism) to spend hours upon hours chasing across
the fields and crawling through the woods? Is it to catch a hare
for dinner or a partridge for supper? Apparently not, because any
poultry shop can supply the most pampered palate with a wide
assortment of game; and to have game on the menu for a whole
week no doubt costs far less than a whole day of hunting with
dogs and loaders. No, what matters for the true lover of the chase
is not to taste or eat game, but to hunt. His passion is for the activity of hunting as such. Eating game is a bonus, but the thrill he
is looking for is the actual chase.

That's how it is with the huntsman, and it is no different
with the angler. Stepping out when it is still half dark, baiting the
hook, lowering the float, and waiting for a nibble, striking at just
the right moment and then landing a pike or a bass, that is the

real pleasure of the recreational fisherman. The sport is the search and the search is the angler's bliss. Buy a fish in the store or receive one as a present, marinated in the finest sauce—that too is a treat; but for a real sportsman nothing can compare with personally angling for a fish in a stream or canal. Our Frisians know how wealthy Englishmen cross over to Frisia just for the pleasure of fishing in the well-stocked Frisian lakes. That is how it is with hunting and fishing, and that is how things stand, though to a lesser degree, for all those who find joy in their daily occupation. Money lightens toil, but money does not inspire. Rembrandt and Frans Hals created marvelous paintings that today are worth their weight in gold, but they were fobbed off with a hundred shillings, if that much. Vondel, our "prince of poets" as he came to be called, worked as a clerk in a hosier's shop and as a teller in a savings and loan bank.[4] Painters who today paint for a living see their talent visibly drying up. But poets and painters who are *artists by the grace of God* are those who write verse because they can't stop themselves and who create paintings because it is their passion. And although this holds especially for artists, it is no less true of our artisans. A mason, a carpenter, a house painter, an upholsterer, if they think only of their weekly pay and derive no pleasure from making things beautiful, from building and upholstering, are not held in high regard by their bosses or their co-workers. Even the farmhand that plows and sows, disks or harrows, should find his enjoyment and passion in the work itself, or his boss will not take him seriously. Small wonder, then, that a real student does not make any progress until the study itself gives him pleasure. The joy of academic life is no longer to have to finish assignments on time, as formerly at school, but to be free to study for the sheer pleasure of it. And the person who graduates and is allowed to assist in the search for truth at a more advanced level, to grope for light in much that is dark and to hunt and dig where no one has

---

4   Kuyper refers in this section to the Dutch painters Rembrandt Harmenszoon van Rijn (1606–69) and Frans Hals (ca. 1581–1666) as well as to Dutch poet and playwright Joost van den Vondel (1587–1679).

gone before, that person relishes his good fortune: he tastes the pleasure of study, indulges his passion with rejoicing, and feels great delight as he engages in *research*.

Accordingly, I have no intention of disputing the delights of seeking after truth. I welcome it with gratitude as a token of God's common grace. When we lost the luxuriance of paradise and were burdened with eating bread by the sweat of our brow, it was a blessing that along with that burden we were given pleasure in work as a spur for that work. A thoroughbred finds pleasure in the race and a pedigree hound takes delight in the chase. A purebred huskie can scarcely be held back from dashing forward. You need a whip only for those animals that lack nobility. To have to till the ground in order to have bread and to plough and sow not slavishly but with joy—that is *grace*. Without passion for work, all that work would debase us. And that the flames of enthusiasm leap even higher when not the hand but the head has to perform the work—that is an even richer gift of grace from God, something which even the pagan poets acknowledged when they explained their irresistible urge from divine inspiration: "Est Deus in nobis, agitant calescimus Illo."[5] It is that wondrous urge to which our generation owes its richest benefits, its greatest treasures. And without doubt it is also true of the pursuit of science that the urge to *seek* truth is from God and that even if you make no discoveries the search itself elevates your person, and that here too *laudanda voluntas*[6] remains a patent of nobility.

With one proviso! Provided science aims to *serve*, never to *rule*. Seeking should be in the service of finding. The ultimate purpose of seeking is finding. Only from this lofty goal does seeking derive its reason for existence. The shepherd who had

---

5   This Latin phrase translates a line from the Roman poet Ovid (ca. 43 BC–ca. AD 17): "There is a god within us, and we glow when stirred by him." Ovid, *Fasti*, bk. 6, line 5.

6   This Latin phrase translates a phrase from a letter written by Ovid to Rufinus, "[Though the power may be lacking,] the will is to be praised," which in the original reads "ut desint vires, tamen est laudanda voluntas." Ovid, *Epistulae ex Ponto*, bk. 3, *Epistle 4: To Rufinus*, line 79.

lost his sheep did not rejoice in searching for it but in finding it; it was then that he called together his friends and neighbors and exclaimed: "Rejoice with me, for I have *found* my sheep."[7] Jesus expressed the same thought about the woman who had lost a piece of silver. And when the prodigal son finally returned home the emphasis was so exclusively on having found him that the father did not mention a word about seeking; he could only shout for joy: "This my son was lost, and is *found*."[8] Delight in searching is priceless, and without it you won't get there; but *finding* must be the goal and motive and therefore the main thing, above all for science that seeks *truth*. When you are really thirsty you do not seek a spring for the sake of seeking but for the water that can slake your thirst; and once you find water, seeking is furthest from your mind. When a traveler through the desert locates a well with bubbling water, he does not withdraw at dusk to forget about its whereabouts, to look for it again the next morning; instead he lies down next to it and falls asleep, to refresh himself with the water at dawn before moving on. Thus when people say that in the field of academic scholarship not the possession of truth, not the finding of truth, but the search for truth is the principal motive, then evidently the thirst for truth has flagged in their hearts and not the desire to possess truth but the pleasure of seeking it is paramount with them. They do not seek in order to find; in fact, too much finding would spoil it for them. The angler who has a bite every minute grows tired of landing fish after fish and no longer finds pleasure in the sport.

And yet, that is all too often how modern scholars approach their studies. They quote the bold words of Lessing: "If God were to hold all Truth concealed in his right hand and in his left only the steady drive to seek Truth but with the proviso that I would forever go astray in the search, and He would bid me choose, I would humbly take the left hand and say: Father, give me this

---

7   Cf. Luke 15:6.

8   Cf. Luke 15:24.

one—the pure Truth is for you alone."[9] Thus for Lessing, the search for truth is more glorious than the possession of truth. But let no one be misled by this pithy saying. For if you say that even Lessing after all did ultimately hope to be in possession of truth provided it were the result of his own searching, that objection does not stand up for one minute. Call truth one hundred, what Lessing's contemporaries knew of it nine, and one-hundredth what he himself along with his adherents could add to it in a life-long search (which is of course far too high an estimate), then it still is true that he would rather die without ever having known nine-tenths of the truth than to have found the truth as a result of his searching for it. Lessing's statement runs perfectly parallel in the intellectual domain to work-righteousness in the moral domain. To want to earn one's own salvation and not receive it by grace is perfectly on a par with the desire to seek all truth by oneself and spurn any revelation of higher light. To prefer to dispense with nine-tenths of the truth rather than to receive the light of truth humbly and gratefully from God's hand is to want to pick from the tree of knowledge in order to be like God and to owe one's knowledge to no one but oneself and to own it thanks solely *to one's own effort*.

You all know the fundamental contrast between knowledge in this life and in the life to come. In this life it is a question of finding by seeking, gradually knowing more and more, but always a knowing *in part* and never otherwise than through a glass, darkly.[10] In eternity, on the other hand, it will always be knowing the essence of things, knowing face to face, knowing God even as we are known by him, a knowing that is immediate, exhaustive, perfect, and for that reason without any *seeking*.[11] And the knowledge which is our possession without seeking

---

9   G. E. Lessing, *Anti-Goetze* (1778), in *Werke,* ed. H. Göpfert (Munich: Carl Hanser Verlag, 1979), 8:32–33.

10 Cf. 1 Cor. 13:12.

11 By this Kuyper means knowing in a qualitative, not quantitative sense.

and which the prophets and apostles say is the most exalted and the most glorious of knowledge—that knowledge is rejected by Lessing and all who follow him, rejected as unworthy of the human spirit. However, those who with us rank the *possession* of truth above all else, and who honor immediate knowledge as the highest knowledge, feel deeply how humbling it would be if we in our sinful state could not gain even the bread of knowledge except "by the sweat of our brow," by dint of our own efforts. We therefore thank our God that all our exertion in seeking after knowledge is attended by delight in studying and that the search itself has its own attraction.

This contrast in standpoint has three direct consequences. If for you the pleasure of seeking truth surpasses the possession of it, then you cause to be lost what is not lost; then you will seek again what others have found long ago; and then you will rather grope in darkness than open your eyes to the light of the revelation that has been given us. If on the other hand you seek only in order to find, you will take care not to lose what you already have; you will no longer seek what was found long ago; and you will gratefully accept what is thrown into your lap without ever having to search for it.

Let us examine each of these three contrasts more closely.

The first contrast is that you must not lose, or cause to be lost, what was not lost to begin with. You know how a cat plays with a mouse: when it has caught the mouse it deliberately lets it go again purely for the pleasure of catching it again. That is how a cat plays, but it does not behoove the man of science to play like that with the truth. All knowledge proceeds from fixed presuppositions, not as artificial hypotheses that fell from the sky but as simple expressions of our existence, of our consciousness, of our perceiving and thinking *I*, including *axioms*, including *perception* as perception and *being* in ourselves, in the cosmos and in that which transcends the senses and is experienced immediately by our soul. This is the common belief that is foundational to all knowledge.

For example, it is by means of discrete numbers and adding, subtracting, multiplying, and dividing them, or taking their square root, that we acquire the sums that we make ourselves by *induction*. But you have to *start* with these discrete numbers; if you commence your computation with zeroes you will always end up with zero. Any lessening of the certainty that is rooted in this fundamental belief can only lead to doubt, to skepticism, and at last to insanity. I do not deny that afterward it is humanity's duty to analyze, plumb, even x-ray the thinking subject. In that respect all of us are in debt to Kant. But analyzing the fact presupposes that the fact is there to begin with. And what is never legitimate is that we imagine that we ourselves have to prove *being itself* and that we willfully discard what we know immediately in order to regain it as the product of our own thinking. The absurd notion of our mind as a tabula rasa began with Descartes, who thought he could make not just knowledge but also being hang by the flimsy threads of an intellectual formula. And ever since Descartes that process of doubt in one form or another has carried on its destructive work without letup. We are no longer sure whether we even have a soul. And if it were not the case that these thinkers, these destroyers of what is immediately given, once outside their ivory towers, time after time deny their own intellectual constructs, then these gentlemen would be of no earthly use in the practical world.

To inspect a precious seal ring that is not lost but that you clasp in your fingers—to assay the karats of its gold and appraise the value of its diamond—is something altogether different from throwing it deliberately into the vortex for the sheer pleasure of retrieving it again. The art of every age mirrors the aspiration and the self-awareness of the age; so it is not an inaccurate characterization when a man of letters, himself a modern of moderns, wondered only recently what the art of the nineteenth century betrays other than an age of feebleness, flabbiness, inconstancy, and insipidity. "Future historians," he exclaims, "will not see anything else in our art but the somber index of the spiritual state of our self-abasing century, the mark of our moral impotence, the melancholy testimony of the bankruptcy of our energies, however much we may boast of our energy."[12] That is the just punishment for people who cause to be lost what they already possessed by casting it into the vortex and who then dive into that vortex in vain hopes of recovering it. As real children of Pilate, they are left with not one fixed starting point for their thinking, not a single pillar in their temple of justice, not one firm rule for their moral code.

For this reason it is not an unscientific standpoint, but a sine qua non for any science which is to enrich humanity, that we in our University resist tooth and nail that wanton rejection of certainty and, honoring religious belief as a foundation also for science and scholarship, use our common sense and hold fast to man's immediate knowing of the basic elements of all being and all thought.

The case is no different with the second contrast that I pointed out: no longer seeking what was long found, or if you will, keeping to our *historical* standpoint over against hypercriticism and its penchant for always starting afresh. The edifice of scholarship is so enormous in design that if the pursuit and practice of science had no order, no collaboration, and no recognition of the historically prepared foundations, the building would never be put under one roof. Then everything that was ever discovered would be lost again and the search each time had to start all over again. Every scholar now living would have to begin afresh, on his own account, and cover the whole field. And every published result would only arouse your suspicion. You would want to look for possible mistakes by former scholars and to show them up for those mistakes. You would claim to be a free, independent

---

12 Leo Claretie in *Le Monde moderne*, no. 68 (August 1900), p. 241.

thinker, and even as a professor you would need to take no notice of anything or anyone. If after ten years you were to topple like a house of cards the results you once dished up with great show of learning, even then, both what you first assembled and what you later discarded would still have to be lauded as "great feats of scholarship."

We refuse to go along with this critical individualism. It is contrary to the very nature and purpose of science. It speaks of the play enjoyed by people who delight in the search, but not of the earnest desire for humanity to advance to ever clearer light of knowledge. If science were concerned with the material world only, with things that can be weighed and measured, there would be no danger in that mania for criticism and that atomistic self-conceit. After all, an experiment can be repeated at the drop of a hat and a mathematical result can be checked at once. But however important the discovery and the manipulation of the forces of nature may be, all disciplines devoted to their study can never yield more than the lower levels of science. You do not ascend to the higher levels of knowledge until you delve into the spiritual sciences of invisible human life and in the relation of that life to the law which it obeys and so to the single mysterious force which causes it to come into being and to pass away again and which directs it to its goal or end. That higher, nobler science is so intricate and complex, and so surpasses what a single century, let alone a single thinker, can encompass, that there can be no question of progress in science unless the next century is prepared to continue spinning the thread as it slips from the failing hands of the dying century. The result of that historical labor has been that this higher science has produced fundamentally different positions which history itself has worked out in blood and tears. Here, subjective differences rule out unity of vision and, depending on a person's mind, one of these historic positions matches that person and that person matches that position. Given that scholars cannot work together unless they share a common starting point, we at this University collaborate exclusively with those who take the position of our Reformed forebears. The way they viewed things strikes us too as the truth—matches the way we too view life. That is why we refuse to take to the streets and put the torch of criticism to everything that has been built up, to start building all over again. We inhabit the Reformed house bequeathed to us by our forebears and that is where we carry on our lives. If that is called *unscientific*, then notice how those who label us with that stigma factually do the same thing, only on less solid grounds. Among them, too, there is not one who has devised his own world of ideas and has investigated every foundation of knowledge. They too float on corks that others have launched in the water. They adjust to the dominant pattern of thinking and simply repeat its slogans. They are Kantians, or Hegelians, or Darwinians, et cetera. They spawn school after school, each with its own catechism, and they swear by the creed of their favorite mentor. Our alphabet has never numbered more than five vowels, and among the critical atomists, too, the consonants, which have never given a sound of their own, account for the bulk of their speech. In other words, they too inhabit a house with others and proceed from a position that others have found. With this difference only, that the position on which we take our stand bears the stamp of centuries, whereas they adjust their kaleidoscope almost every decade. Plus this difference as well: we for our part *openly acknowledge* that we proceed from what others have found, whereas they deceive themselves by claiming that they never come out with anything other than fresh produce from their own greenhouse.

The third point I indicated is even more important. The first was, not to cause to be lost what is not lost to begin with and therefore to maintain the elementary things that are sensed through immediate knowledge. The second was our historical standpoint: not to seek again what others already found long ago.

Now to add the third point: stop seeking if God graciously reveals to you what you were seeking.

This too is a reasonable demand. The opposite is the way of the schoolboy who has to practice his arithmetic. Even though the answers to the problems he is assigned are in the back of the book, still he has to find them for himself. And that makes perfectly good sense in his case, since the problems themselves are never taken seriously by him. His goal is to *learn* arithmetic. But if you could cable Lord Roberts the current whereabouts of De Wet,[13] the fox would not for a moment consider tearing up your telegram without first reading it simply for the pleasure of continuing the search. And that is how it is in every domain. When someone is roaming the mountains and just cannot find the right path, he is delighted when he meets a guide who can show him the way; and he would make himself ridiculous if he were nevertheless to say to the guide, "I won't listen to you because I want to go on looking for the path myself." No captain of a ship that is driven off course will, when hailed by a pilot's boat, hoist all sails and steer clear of the pilot in order to look for the course himself. To continue searching when someone else brings you what you are looking for is contrary to everything that is reasonable, and what is unreasonable should not be called scientific.

So here. Science, too, encounters questions in life that scientists never give up trying to solve but without ever solving them. Whence the origin of things? Who rules this world and gave the world its law for life? What differentiates organic life from mechanics? Whence sin? Is there life after death? How can right triumph over might? How is reconciliation possible? Where is the unity of history in the multiplicity of events? And so on and so forth. All of them are questions that continue to exercise the human mind, and the answers to these questions determine our

---

13 Frederick Roberts, 1st Earl Roberts (1832–1914), and Christiaan de Wet (1854–1922) were opposing generals in the Second Boer War (1899–1902), which was in progress at the time this address was given.

energy, our courage to face life, the motive of our supreme devotion, the peace of our heart, and our heroism in the face of death. Nevertheless, all that questioning, all that searching is useless. Results have remained as scanty as thirty centuries ago in India, Greece, or China. But now God has revealed himself. He has spoken in a variety of ways to the fathers through his prophets and apostles.[14] He sent us the One who said, "I am the way, and the truth, and the life."[15] He has sealed his faithfulness to us in his Word. And He continues to call out to all who seek but never find: "Come, everyone who thirsts, come to the waters; and he who has no money, come, buy and eat! Come, buy wine and milk without money and without price."[16] Or to speak with the learned scholar from Tarsus: "For since, in the wisdom of God, the world did not know God through wisdom, it pleased God through the folly of what we preach to save [i.e., to enrich, also in knowledge] those who believe."[17] Thanks to this revelation a generation arose that no longer wavered in fear nor sought in vain, but that dared to say: "We know."[18] It was a generation that possessed certainty and whose firmness of conviction enabled them to show forth invincible power. Earlier, Jesus had said of these heroes of firm conviction: "I thank you, Father, that you have hidden these things from the wise and understanding and revealed them to little children"[19]—i.e., unto those who are willing to be children in matters of the spirit.

Where do we see here, I do not say erudition, but true science that aims at genuine knowledge? Is it found in the vain groping and guessing of those who mock this revelation and keep on searching without ever getting beyond agnosticism? Or is it found

---

14 Cf. Heb. 1:1.

15 John 14:6.

16 Isa. 55:1.

17 1 Cor. 1:21; bracketed insertion by the author.

18 1 John 3:14.

19 Cf. Luke 10:21.

in our standpoint, whereby we gratefully accept the God-given solution to those profound questions and through our studies continue to build with boldness and inspiration on the foundation laid by the prophets and the apostles.

Now, all this is governed by the fundamental question I raised at the outset: *What is the goal of genuine study?* Is the goal of science to open up a hunting ground for a few scholars to indulge in their critical investigations, or is it to endow people with certainty, firmness of conviction, *knowledge?* And if it follows from this, assuming you opt for the latter, that to cause to be lost what was not lost, to search anew for what our forebears already found, and to keep on seeking what God has revealed cannot possibly be reconciled with a reasonable understanding of science's goal, why then, from the point of view of science, is the standpoint of the Free University objected to when it favors thirst for truth above the pleasure of study, finding above seeking, and when it thus upholds both immediate knowledge, results once obtained, and the solution given in God's Word to otherwise insoluble questions?

———— ❀ ————

But we are not there yet. Our threefold starting point may be vindicated, but it is not yet clear what scientific studies are meant to do. The immediate pronouncements of one's consciousness come naturally; the guiding principles of the Calvinist worldview are more or less known; the answers that God's Word offers for the great questions of life are summed up in the Apostles' Creed. So what is left for science to do?

My answer is that science is to fulfill the threefold task that constitutes the calling of every university: first, to establish; second, to deduce; and third, to systematize. Science is to establish the wealth of truth that we acquire either immediately or by induction. Next, it is to deduce from these firm data the implications for our present life and our current state of consciousness.

And finally, science is to take this wealth of truth and its implications and bring them into coherence, i.e., raise them into a system. I will not detain you with a discussion of the last two tasks. No one suspects the seriousness with which we at the Free University work at these tasks, nor does it occur to anyone to dispute, given our declared standpoint, our right or our ability to deduce and systematize in keeping with the rules of science. We stand for three principles—certainty of our consciousness, historic Calvinism, and Scriptural revelation—from which implications for every relationship in life can be deduced with logical rigor. Likewise, no man of science can resist the urge through systematization to elucidate the essential coherence of his principles and the organic link of his various deductions to those principles. Thus I have never heard that where our deductions and our systematization are concerned the scientific nature of our work is disqualified.

But I strongly emphasize that first task: establishing the wealth of truth from which we proceed. That is the point where we are attacked. The allegation is that we certify unproven assumptions arbitrarily, hence unscientifically, and that we merely parrot traditional dogmas. Exactly here lies the misunderstanding. On the contrary, establishing the truths we possess demands wide-ranging studies that penetrate to the root of the matter. Not as though we would still want to *prove* the certainty of the axiomatic pronouncements of our consciousness. That would be a contradiction in terms. No school of thought entertains such an absurd argument. Even Descartes took his *cogito* as a *given* starting point and tried from there to ascend to his *ergo sum*. And, inversely, it is no secret for us either how easily a *common opinion* that is accepted for a time in certain circles can be mistaken for the immediate pronouncement of our consciousness. What is real has to be separated from what is imagined, and to be able to do so we have to investigate the nature of this certainty, explain it psychologically, and confine it to the elementary givens. We confess, more than other schools, that false lines have been drawn across our immediate consciousness by the darkening effect of sin. Thus the allegation is simply ludicrous that we believe having a firm starting point excuses us from examining it more closely.

The case is no different with respect to our historical principle. Or do people think that the Reformed worldview has been slipped into our hands in a secret document, ready to hand and fully worked out? Is Calvinism in its rise and flowering not a historical phenomenon which just like any other configuration in history has to be mined from the sources? And does finding its leading idea not require that we remove its time-bound features, separate the leaven from the flour, and trace the unity behind its multiple forms? And if this is as clear as day, why should establishing the Reformed principle be judged less scientific than establishing the spirit of India or Greece?

And the case is again no different when we come to the principle of revelation from Scripture. Here too it is an altogether false idea that Scripture offers a ready confession and a cut-and-dried catechism for life. What Scripture reveals can only be established after thorough study. And although *belief* in the truth of Scripture is a fruit of the *testimonium Spiritus Sancti*, which is surer than anything else, *knowledge* of Scripture and its contents can only be the fruit of study and research. So much so, in fact, that there is no book in any language that has been subjected to more thoroughgoing, comprehensive, and unremitting study than Holy Scripture.

For us too, therefore, establishing the truth that we possess has nothing in common with drawing up an inventory of known truths without having to do any serious scholarship. On the contrary, only psychological, historical, and biblical studies that go to the root of things can enable us to establish in an informed way just what we possess. Our certainty of consciousness needs psychological study; our Calvinist standpoint needs historical study; the revelation of our God needs biblical study. This is all the more important since by far not all Christian thinkers reach the same conclusions as we do, either now or in former centuries. On each of the three topics mentioned, divergent schools of thought have arisen leading to friction and controversy. And this controversy, in which we are obliged to demonstrate the soundness of our conclusions over and over again, compels us continually to test and inspect *the way we establish* what we know, an inspection that does not spare a single detail.

But even then the task of establishing is still not complete. Non-Christians and anti-Christians time and again allege that much of what we store in our treasury of truth as gold and diamonds is tinsel and paste. Now nothing is further from our mind than to say that we couldn't care less what others say about us. Our bond with our fellow citizens is felt deeply by us and includes those among them who oppose us. Science and scholarship is a common human endeavor and he who shuts himself up within his own circle without ever "having it out" with those who think otherwise leaves the refreshing stream and ends up in a stagnant bog. We have to engage the objections of those who oppose us on principle and to attack their notions that we deem false—attack them, not in bitter hatred, but from love of those who are misled by them.

Only, we go about this with level heads and a discriminating eye. So long as our strength is so little and so much still needs to be done to build our own house, we shall concentrate our energies first of all on the positive, deductive, and systematic investigation of our principles. How we divide our time and energy is our decision. If you rush to spend all your time as an apologist, you will always lose in influence, you will be mostly disappointed by a poor reception and a poor outcome, and you will have your studies dictated to you by your opponent. Your studies will lose focus, and every morning you will have to be ready to answer what has been brought against you this time. You will be tied down by an unproductive series of ad hoc arguments. That first of all. And then in the second place, we refuse to waste our energy refuting for the umpteenth time what has so often been refuted already. Many of the objections raised against us are worn-out theses that have been fully answered long ago. Staging a gladiator's match too frequently makes it unpalatable: it is *oleum et operam perdere*.[20] And one more thing, in the third place. By far the majority of these objections are inferences from contrary premises that are governed by a philosophical idea. Now it is always fundamentally *unscientific* to wage the battle in the area of inferences so long as the starting premises have not been thrashed out. Why engage in an argument, for example, about Christian doctrine with someone who denies it, so long as you haven't come to agreement on the authority of Scripture? Or again, why argue with that person about the authority of Scripture so long as you haven't agreed on the meaning of the concepts of sin and revelation? But although on that account sound scientific method indeed demands that you settle an argument about the source of a river high up in the mountains and not down by the seashore, nevertheless where the fundamental premises are at issue we too have to join battle, even in the case of a Nietzsche. A scientific school that declines to give account of itself commits suicide.

Thus we do not in any way shirk the strict demand that scientific verification should extend to the most critical level. Not that we close our eyes to subjective differences in fundamental convictions. Aesthetically you will never convince a deaf person of the beauty of Beethoven's symphonies. Ethically a Nero could never be convinced of the sacredness of marriage. Similarly, in the domain of truth Jesus judged that "unless one is born of water and the Spirit, he cannot even *see* the kingdom of God."[21] But even then that subjective element itself remains open to scientific debate, and we are prepared in that respect to demonstrate the legitimacy of our standpoint.

---

20 This Latin phrase means a waste of time and trouble. See Plautus, *Poenulus*, act 1, scene 2, line 333.

21 Cf. John 3:3, 5, which Kuyper conflates here as a paraphrase.

——————∘⁂∘——————

Assuming that this is so—that we are obliged and prepared, at least at a time of our own choosing, to give an account of everything, even of our deepest convictions—if you should now ask, finally, in what way we differ from others and why we concentrate our studies in a university of our own (after all, one can debate about certainty of consciousness, Calvinism, and Scripture at any university), then this is my threefold answer. The first is that although the state universities are said to be religiously neutral and admit every opinion to their forum, the fact is that for many years already only one school of thought has set the tone, and even Bilderdijk, Groen van Prinsterer, and Da Costa[22] were debarred from their faculties. In the second place, the university also aims to form and mold its students. Now then, pedagogically speaking, an education that calls a lie in Tuesday's lecture what was recommended in Monday's lecture as the truth mocks the primordial demands of a formative education. Moreover—and this I want to note in the last place—there is proof and proof. There is a kind of proof that settles the question once for all. But there is also a kind of proof which, when it fails to convince or even when it fails outright, nevertheless in your eyes leaves unimpaired the truth that was truth for you before the proof was ever undertaken. A judge does not accept the truth of a fact until the evidence submitted is complete; what is not proven adequately he may never accept as truth nor act on it. But that your mother is your mother and that you were begotten by your father is so much part and parcel of your experience of life that the fear of being a baby switched at birth or a child born of adultery *can* never enter your heart. You never searched for a document to prove it. But suppose an inheritance has to be divided

---

22 Poet Willem Bilderdijk (1756–1831), politician and historian Guillaume Groen van Prinsterer (1801–76), and Netherlands-born messianic Jewish poet Isaäc da Costa (1798–1860) were early nineteenth-century pioneers of the Calvinist revival (*Réveil*) in the Netherlands.

and an evil person fastens suspicion on your family connection, then you won't sit still; then you hunt down whatever proof you can find. But even if you did not succeed in that, the truth of the matter would never be shaken in your mind. And this difference holds also here. Every rationalist wants to put you in the dock, and in the absence of proof that in *his* eyes is complete he will contest your right to hold your conviction. Now when you face such a denial you too will collect all the evidence available to you and argue your case as thoroughly and powerfully as you can, but also in such a way that you firmly believe the truth of your own basic conviction not *after but before* the debate takes place. In fact, even if the debate is called off, that basic conviction is still not weakened in your soul by a millionth of a milligram. This is not just so among us, but among all men of principle. Everyone's basic conviction is the axiom of one's self-consciousness that will defy every wave of attack: *saevis tranquillum in undis.*[23]

———— ⊸⟞⊸ ————

So long as your own consciousness, therefore, is not a mirror that by turns reflects every color, but has a center that sends out its own strong searchlight, two things will stand out: first, your basic conviction has nothing to fear from the most thorough investigation; and second, our basic conviction actually demands that all scientific research should go down to the root of the matter. And therefore, as resolutely as we reject the scholarly pride of a Lessing, who organized the pursuit for truth merely for the pleasure of the pursuit, so strongly do we urge you to pursue your studies with scientific rigor, but only on condition that *thirst for truth* be your incentive.

Am I reassured about that? Allow me to share an observation with you. At other universities I have sometimes noticed, especially among theology students, a measure of enthusiasm for

---

23 This Latin phrase is translated, "Calm amid the fierce waves."

study that I have often missed among you. But what was it that accounted for that impulse at those other schools? The impulse arose from the passion to *negate,* to contribute personally, if possible, toward prying loose a stone from the walls of God's holy Zion that was still held in place. It arose from the critical spirit to outstrip others in unraveling the Christian confession. What accounted for this drive and incentive was the impulse of a spiritual vandalism that will not rest until the last pillar is pulled down. That is how those students joined the ranks of the intellectual iconoclasts, how they became a little Strauss, a miniature Bauer, and how they dreamt of being a disciple of Renan.[24] For this they reaped approval and praise. Their professors gratefully drafted them into the light cavalry of the elite army of critics. Their name sometimes became known in other countries. Such *promising* young men! And that goad did wonders, for in our younger years—why deny it?—we have a lot of untamed energy; moreover, a revolutionary trait runs through every scholar's soul, and joining in something brand-new can cast a dangerous spell. Oh, those innovators of yesterday! Such laurels will not be reaped by you. We do not train you in demolishing what is standing, nor are we set up for that. As well, our respect for the holy is too powerful not to label these attacks on God's truth as sacrilege and so appeal to the conscience of those who perpetrate them. No, if the spirit of study is to awaken more strongly *among you,* then your motive must not be self-exaltation but the exaltation of the glory of God, and your focus is to be on shoring up whatever is tottering. Then your critical exactness must be balanced by your historical sense. Then in your estimation Augustine must rise high above Strauss, and Aquinas far above Renan, and not Wellhausen's creeping tendrils but the laurel sprays of Voetius

---

24 German theologian and philosopher David Friedrich Strauss (1808–74), German philosopher and historian Bruno Bauer (1809–82), and French philologist and historian Ernest Renan (1823–92) were pioneers of biblical criticism in the middle of the nineteenth century as well as writers on the life of Jesus from a naturalistic standpoint.

should keep sleep from your eyes. Then the passion of your soul should be for God, for His cause, and what should rouse you to holy jealousy is to wipe away skepticism and negation from the pavement of his holy temple, even if only from a single stone in it. That will not be easy. To declare a psalm to be Maccabean or excise another chapter out of Isaiah is much more clever, and the cheerleaders from the gallery of critics will start applauding even before you have finished. And yet, I know, you will not shirk this holy task. Soon it will become apparent among you that thirst for truth is a more powerful motive for study than the appetite for negation. The love of God's people will compensate you for the applause that will pass you by. And the God of truth, whose honor laid hold of you, will, if you have not forgotten the holy art of prayer, sharpen your mental powers, enhance your talent, and in his holy name will make you succeed.

There are already quite a few who have graduated from your noble circle. May many of you in our audience today follow in their footsteps. Let the academic year begin! May it do its part in contributing toward that lofty goal, and let us take up our studies tomorrow as those who know that only that which is begun with God has meaning for eternity.

I thank you.

ABOUT THE ABRAHAM KUYPER
TRANSLATION SOCIETY

In 2011 a group of Abraham Kuyper scholars and experts met to form an association that has come to be known as the Abraham Kuyper Translation Society. Kuyper College and Acton Institute, along with other Abraham Kuyper scholars, have an interest in facilitating the translation of Abraham Kuyper's writings into English. Currently the society is involved in translating Kuyper's seminal three-volume work on common grace (*De gemeene gratie*), his three-volume work on the lordship of Christ (*Pro rege*), and key Kuyper texts on the church. The translated texts on the church will be published by Christian's Library Press as an anthology.

The society recognizes that translations are not ends in themselves. Hence, plans are underway to produce an Abraham Kuyper Islam anthology that will focus on how deeply Kuyper's encounter with Islam toward the end of his life affected him and galvanized *Pro rege*, the last major work Kuyper completed in religion and theology. One anticipated result of translating Kuyper's writings on Islam is to reveal to twenty-first century Christians, particularly Christian students, how Kuyper successfully "engaged" another world religion and another culture. It is also hoped that this anthology, along with the translation of Kuyper's other writings, will enable Christians to draw on their Reformation heritage and develop a sense of vocation as wide as creation itself.

The society also exists to further additional Kuyper scholarly projects that will help promote a holistic vision of God's renewal encompassing all things.

ACTON INSTITUTE | KUYPER 🍃 COLLEGE

ABOUT ABRAHAM KUYPER

(1837–1920)

Abraham Kuyper's life began in the small Dutch village of Maas-sluis on October 29, 1837. During his first pastorate, he developed a deep devotion to Jesus Christ, spurring him to a deep commit-ment to Reformed theology, which profoundly influenced his later careers. He labored tirelessly, publishing two newspapers, leading a reform movement out of the state church, founding the Free University of Amsterdam, and serving as prime minister of the Netherlands. He died on November 8, 1920, after relentlessly endeavoring to integrate his faith and life; truly, his emphasis on worldview formation has had a transforming influence upon evangelicalism, through the diaspora of the Dutch Reformed churches and those they have inspired.

In the mid-nineteenth-century Dutch political arena, the in-creasing sympathy for the "No God, no master!" dictum of the French Revolution greatly concerned Kuyper. To desire freedom from an oppressive government or a heretical religion was one thing, but to eradicate religion from politics as spheres of mu-tual influence was, for Kuyper, unthinkable. Because man is sin-ful, he reasoned, a state that derives its power from men cannot avoid the vices of fallen human impulses. True limited government flourishes best when people recognize their sinful condition and acknowledge God's divine authority. In Kuyper's words, "The sovereignty of the state as the power that protects the individual and that defines the mutual relationships among the visible spheres, rises high above them by its right to command and compel. But within these spheres . . . another authority rules, an authority that descends directly from God apart from the state. This authority the state does not confer but acknowledges."

ABOUT THE TRANSLATOR

Harry Van Dyke was born in Rotterdam, Holland, and at the age of twelve moved with his parents and six siblings to Canada. He earned a BA at Calvin College and a DLitt at the VU University Amsterdam. He has published a score of articles, numerous translations, and a book, *Groen van Prinsterer's Lectures on Unbelief and Revolution* (1989), besides editing anthologies of the writings of S. U. Zuidema and M. C. Smit.

For twelve years he served as research fellow and instructor in theory and philosophy of history at the VU University Amsterdam, and then taught history in Redeemer University College for twenty-three years. Since his retirement he has given direction to the Dooyeweerd Centre for Christian Philosophy and has been involved in several translation projects. He and his wife have two adult daughters and two grandchildren, and they reside in Hamilton, Ontario, where they are members of one of five local Christian Reformed churches

Made in USA - North Chelmsford, MA
1383170_9781938948855
09.06.2023 1521